Financial Advice:

The Top Building Blocks to Personal Wealth and Financial Independence

© **Copyright 2016 by Ben Collins - All rights reserved.**

The follow eBook is reproduced below with the goal of providing information that is as accurate and reliable as possible. Regardless, purchasing this eBook can be seen as consent to the fact that both the publisher and the author of this book are in no way experts on the topics discussed within and that any recommendations or suggestions that are made herein are for entertainment purposes only. Professionals should be consulted as needed prior to undertaking any of the action endorsed herein.

This declaration is deemed fair and valid by both the American Bar Association and the Committee of Publishers Association and is legally binding throughout the United States.

Furthermore, the transmission, duplication or reproduction of any of the following work including specific information will be considered an illegal act irrespective of if it is done electronically or in print. This extends to creating a secondary or tertiary copy of the work or a recorded copy and is only allowed with express written consent from the Publisher. All additional right reserved.

The information in the following pages is broadly considered to be a truthful and accurate account of facts and as such any inattention, use or misuse of the information in question by the reader will render any resulting actions solely under their purview. There are no scenarios in which the publisher or the original author of this work can be in any fashion deemed liable for any hardship or damages that may befall them after undertaking information described herein.

Additionally, the information in the following pages is intended only for informational purposes and should thus be thought of as universal. As befitting its nature, it is presented without assurance regarding its prolonged validity or interim quality. Trademarks that are mentioned are done without written consent and can in no way be considered an endorsement from the trademark holder.

Table of Contents

Introduction 1

Chapter 1: The Mindset of Financially Independent Individuals 2

Chapter 2: Taxation Basics 6

Chapter 3: Putting Inflation to Work for You 9

Chapter 4: Investing Overview 12

Chapter 5: Managing Risk 16

Chapter 6: Setting the Right Goals 19

Conclusion 22

Introduction

Congratulations on downloading *Financial Advice: The Top Building Blocks to Personal Wealth and Financial Independence* and thank you for doing so. When it comes to preparing for your future, there are few things that you can do that are more effective for your long term success and happiness than securing your financial independence. In these uncertain economic times this is easier said than done, however, which is why this book was created to help you know where to start and to get up and running on the surest, and shortest, path to success.

To that end, the following chapters will discuss everything you need to know in order to get on your way when it comes to creating enough personal wealth to one day realistically be able to plan for financial independence. This starts with understanding the mindset of those who are already on their way to being financially independent and how it naturally differs from the mindset of those who can't seem to get out of the mentality that causes them to live paycheck to paycheck month after month and year after year. You will then learn how to take advantage of the system like the millionaires do by taking as many credits and deductions on your federal taxes as humanly possible and putting the natural force of inflation to work for you on all of your investments.

When it comes to investments, you will also learn everything you need to know about the primary investment types and how to go about taking the first steps towards investing in each. More importantly, you will also learn how to manage the risk level on your investments so that you never get burned too badly and how to set the right goals to ensure success in both the short and the long term.

There are plenty of books on this subject on the market, thanks again for choosing this one! Every effort was made to ensure it is full of as much useful information as possible, please enjoy!

Chapter 1: The Mindset of Financially Independent Individuals

When it comes to achieving financial independence, it is easy for those who are on the outside looking in to assume there is some universal secret that is keeping them forever on the outside. The reality of the situation is that instead of there being one big secret, there are numerous small differences between those who are financially secure and those who are forever living paycheck to paycheck. This starts with mindset that those who are financially independent cultivate and the habits that they tend to exhibit.

Mindset

No matter the situation that you currently find yourself in, there is a path that you can find that will take you to where you want to be when it comes to financial freedom. That path might not always be easy, or clearly marked, but with the right mindset it is always going to be eventually attainable. While certain aspects of a financially independent existence may sometimes more naturally lead to certain mindsets, they are by no means qualifications for them. Consider the following examples of a financially independent mindset versus a paycheck to paycheck mindset and consider what you can do to ensure that you change from one to the other.

Financially independent mindset: I can change my circumstances

Paycheck to paycheck mindset: My circumstances define me

While those who are already financially independent may find this lesson easier to learn, the truth of the matter is that no matter what situation you currently find yourself in, you can improve if you simply take the time to work out a plan that is realistic and then stick to it with a thorough resolve that will not wear thin no matter what. While there are certainly financial holes that you can find yourself in that may seem too deep to ever emerge from, the truth of the matter is that diligence is the only thing you need to have in your possession if you hope to change your place in the world.

Currently there are more self-made millionaires and billionaires in the United States than there have ever been before. Anyone with a good idea and a little programming skill can make an application that becomes a best seller, anyone with a good idea for a blog can become a household name and anyone with an idea for a teen romance story with some supernatural or science fiction elements can be an overnight sensation. The truth of the matter is that the only thing holding you back is your ability to dream big and commit to making that dream a reality. Believe that anything is possible and you will already be on your way.

Financially independent mindset: Through planning my dreams will come true

Paycheck to paycheck mindset: Dreams are meant to be flights of fancy

While learning to take your dreams seriously is one thing, making a concentrated effort to work towards them is what separates those who earn their financial independence and those who forever find themselves living paycheck to paycheck. The truth of the matter is that it is easy to think about becoming financially independent as a flight of fancy, but it is much harder to do so in terms of what you can do, step by step, in order to make it a reality. As such, you are going to want to start with your ultimate dream before working backwards until you find the first goal you will need to accomplish that you can actively begin working towards. Once you finish that first goal, move on to the second and don't stop until you are staring back on where you have come from in surprise.

Financially independent mindset: I am going to get started today

Paycheck to paycheck mindset: I will find time to get started someday soon

While those who are already financially independent will often have an easier time finding time to getting started on a new goal, feeling as though your time is already spread thin is no excuse when it comes to changing your life for the better. It doesn't matter what your schedule currently consists of, if you ever hope to change your lot in life then you have to be willing to put in the time to make those dreams a reality. What's worse, planning on starting someday soon, or someday when you have more time, is actually worse than not having semi-concrete plans as vague goals will only serve to keep you pacified with the current state of things, and pacified is not a state that you can afford to be in.

Financially independent mindset: Failure is a part of the process

Paycheck to paycheck mindset: Staying put is better than trying and failing

If you find yourself having a hard time getting started, simply because the thought of failure seems as though it is too much to handle, this is likely caused by a deeply rooted dichotomy that everyone on earth is a part of. There are two types of people in the world, those with a growth mindset and those with a fixed mindset. Those with a growth mindset were told at a young age that they succeed when they but their minds to something and work through it, and as a result they ultimately learned to take pleasure in overcoming challenges and expanding their horizons. While these types of people can still be stymied by other types of negative mindsets, they have no problem looking at failure as something to be overcome.

On the other hand, those who were told at a young age that they succeeded because they were special or because of some innate amount of strength, perception, endurance, charisma, intelligence, agility, luck or some combination of the punch developed a fixed mindset which made them more likely to appreciate the idea of appearing to be something regardless of the truth of the matter. Those with a fixed mindset then find it difficult to overcome roadblocks in their path that cannot be overcome with an initial application of force. Once they have been rebuffed they are more likely to favor avoidance, a tactic that is untenable when it comes to being financially independent. Luckily, those with a fixed mindset can shift to a beneficial growth mindset by being aware of their nature and making an active effort to try and be different; with enough time new neural pathways will form and habits will change.

Chapter 2: Taxation Basics

When it comes to ensuring that you are able to legally keep as much of the money that you do earn each calendar year as possible, it helps to have a clear idea of just what the United States tax code asks of you when it comes to your federal income tax instead of blindly going into tax season willing to pay every penny that it appears you owe at first blush. As of 2016, the various tax brackets, ranked lowest to highest, start at 10 percent and increase to 15 percent, 25 percent, 28 percent, 33 percent, 35 percent and 39.6 percent. To be taxed at 10 percent you need to make $9,000 or less in a given year before taxes, to be taxed at 25 percent you will need to be single and making $85,000 per year before taxes and to be taxed at 39.6 percent you need to be making $500,000 or more each year before taxes.

Nontaxable income: The simple fact of the matter is that all income is not created equal in the eyes of the federal government which is why so many monies individuals have so many types of investments. There are numerous types of income that fall under this qualification, some of the most common include:

- Municipal bonds are bonds that are put out at a local level and are well known for having interest that is accrued tax free. While these bonds tend to generate a smaller amount of overall return, that return is not taxed which makes it the right choice for those looking to reduce their federal tax penalties in certain situations.

- Any disability benefits that come from an insurance policy that you pay for yourself can also be collected tax free as are some social security benefits assuming your overall income falls within the required levels.

- Those who work abroad do not need to pay federal income taxes as long as they make less than $98,000 in a calendar year. If you have to pay an income tax in the country that you are residing in at the time the work is completed, you will also get a credit for that amount on your US tax return.

- Long term capital gains returns can reach a 0 percent rate for individuals in the 10 and 15 percent tax brackets. For example, a couple who makes $72,500 a year would not have to pay capital gains taxes, nor would an individual who makes less than $36,500 a year.

Credits: Aside from nontaxable income, you may find it useful to take a closer look at all of the various credits that you could possibly be qualified to take without even realizing it.

- A married couple with two children can earn a maximum of nearly $30,000 by going through their expenses line by line or at least $12,200 for their children and $3,900 a piece for themselves. If the family also falls into certain tax brackets they can then qualify for the earned income credit which pays out as much as $6,000. If both parents then work and they have to pay someone else to take care of their children who are under the age of 13, then they can earn $6,000 more.

- The American opportunity credit provides as much as $2,500 each year for students who qualify while the saver's credit provides the same amount for those who earn a moderate income and are trying to save for the future.

Deductions: Deductions are amounts that are taken out of your income prior to the amount that you owe in taxes being calculated which means you will have to pay less in taxes while still using those funds for a wide variety of purposes. It is important to speak with a tax professional in order to ensure you get all the deductions each year that you possibly can. Possible deductions include:

- Cash donations or donations of property that go to many different charitable organizations can often be deducted from your income for the year.

- Mortgage interest can often be deducted assuming it is on a loan on the residence that you primarily occupy. This can also include things like a home equity loan, home equity credit line or a first or second mortgage.

- Profits generated from any type of retirement account or company IRA will also have the ability to be deducted with a contribution limit that is $5,500 for those under the age of 50 and $6,500 for those over the age of 50.

- If you purchased a brand new car in a calendar year then you often deduct the amount that you paid in sales tax, even if you otherwise don't choose to itemize your deductions. This deduction is not available to those whose yearly income exceeds $135,000.

- If you own your home and decide to make one or more of any number of green improvement you can see significant federal deductions of $1,500 or more.

- You are allowed to deduct the mileage that you have driven to volunteer for a cause if it is a significant distance. You will be allowed to deduct the standard rate for this commute, as well as any childcare costs that you had to pay in order to participate in the event in question. If the purpose of the volunteering was mentoring through programs like Big Sisters or Big Brothers, then you are also allowed to deduct various expenses such as tickets to events or meals purchased while out and about. This doesn't include money that you spent for your own participation in said events, just the mentee.

- Business related entertainment and meals can all be deducted which can seriously add up if you own your own business and find yourself having to wine and dine prospective clients simply because this is the way that things are done. It is important to keep all of these costs separate from your personal costs, though you do count your own expenses in with the deduction. In this instance you are allowed to deduct half of the cost of every business meal and the full cost of any business entertainment.

- When medical expenses exceed 10 percent of your gross income then they can often be deducted as long as they are itemized. This includes things like capital improvements that are made with accommodation in mind after a serious accident or onset of a medical condition.

Chapter 3: Putting Inflation to Work for You

Inflation can be thought of as a long term increase in the consumer cost of various goods and services that occurs naturally over time. While as a consumer, inflation is never going to be your ally, as an investor it can make you quite a pretty penny when you know how to utilize it properly. This is because inflation naturally erodes the currency value of a given country, for example a gallon of milk used to cost only $1 instead of $4 which means that if you take out a loan to purchase one of the inflation hedges below then you will be able to pay for your investment with money that is worth less than the money you borrowed originally. There are numerous factors that influence the rate of inflation but the end result is always going to be people who are willing to pay more for the same result.

As an investor, it is easy for you to find an investment that is likely to increase in value at a rate that exceeds the general inflation rate and typically includes things like stocks, bonds that are inflation indexed, oil, gold and real estate (discussed more in the next chapter). The various types of investments are discussed from an inflation angle below, but it is important to do more research on the type of inflation hedge you are considering before going ahead and pulling the trigger. Each type of investment hedge has its owns pros and cons and it is important to have a clear idea of what these entail before making a decision.

What's more, like all investments it is important to keep in mind that you have no guarantees when it comes to the success of your choice, as there are specific, if relatively rare, conditions that the market can reach where they tend to perform worse than they otherwise might, just as there are scenarios where they will exceed expectations. As such, even when dealing with what is virtually guaranteed to be a sure thing you are never going to want to make an investment you can't afford to walk away from at a moment's notice.

Investments to profit from inflation

Real estate: When it comes to inflation, real estate is often considered to be the most popular choice when it comes to inflation hedges as it can allow the owner to generate rental income for years while letting the value of the property mature as well. What's more, the rate you can charge

Gold: Gold is also often used these days as a way to hedge against inflation as it is often purchased in greater degrees during times of economic uncertainty when inflation is often known to rise. While other precious metals will typically gain value in the same way, gold is the headliner, the precious metal all the occasional investors think of, and will always be the one to benefit from instances of inflation to the greatest degree.

Oil: Oil is a useful investment during periods of inflation as gasoline is often one of the first commodities hit with price increases which filter back to oil prices eventually causing them to outpace the going rate of inflation at almost all turns.

Stock: Stock can be useful for warding off inflation assuming the underlying companies manage to pass the excess costs off to their consumers. The fluid nature of stock also makes it easy to sell of minimal losses should that turn out to not be the case. Current studies put the two products that people will continue to buy no matter the cost increase are toilet paper and toothpaste, do with that what you will.

Treasury Inflation Protected Securities: Treasury Inflation Protected Securities are one of the most popular types of bonds that are indexed in regards to inflation. This means that unlike traditional bonds it doesn't decrease in value over time as inflation increases. Also known as TIPS, this type of protected security is tied to the Consumer Price Index which is the primary way of determining the average for what are known as a basket of consumer services or goods. Various different baskets include things like medical care, food or transportation and the average is determined by calculating the price changes connected to various items in the basket and then average out the total. Changes to the Consumer Price Index are primarily used when it comes to determining the changes in price that are related to the cost of living.

As the Consumer Price Index increases, the value of any TIPS investments you have made will increase as well. The base value for the TIPS will increase as the index increases which means the amount of your return will increase as inflation increases. There are also versions of bonds that are adjusted for inflation that are issued by various countries around the world.

Other inflation hedges: While they are used in this way less often than the options discussed above, high-yield debt and bank loans are both considered solid choices which it comes to creating an investment hedge against inflation. Bank loans are what are known as floating-rate instruments, this means that the bank has the ability to increase the interest rate to ensure the return on investment stays apace with the current rate of inflation. Meanwhile, debt that is considered high-yield can be counted on in most cases to gain values as inflation increase which cause investors to look to buying up the debt of others.

Chapter 4: Investing Overview

Stocks: Buying stock in a company is akin to purchasing a small ownership share of the company in question which means that you may be entitled to dividends when the stock performs well in addition to voting rights on the board leadership in some cases. Stocks can be extremely volatile which means that while the reward if things go your way can be quite substantial, the odds that it will do so are far from guaranteed. One of the biggest benefits of stocks is that there are so many different ways to invest in them and still return a profit. It doesn't matter if you are buying or selling, if you have a personalized trading plan that works for you then you can make money in the stock market if you are willing to work at it.

If you are interested in investing in stocks but want something that is a bit more stable than the traditional market, then you may be interested in investing in indexes instead. An index is a portfolio, or collection, of stocks that are a reflection of some part of the market as a whole. The most commonly known indexes are the Dow Jones Industrial Average and the Nasdaq Composite Index. The Dow Jones is made up of the 30 biggest publicly traded companies in the US and the Nasdaq contains more than 3,000 companies from primarily the internet and technology sectors. While the companies in the Nasdaq are known to have a higher growth potential, the companies in the Dow Jones are known to return extremely reliable results.

Bonds: Typically lumped together under the category of what are called fixed income securities, the term bond can be used to refer to any type of security that is created based on debt. If you choose to purchase a bond, what you are really doing is giving your money to a particular government or company in exchange for a set amount of interest over a prolonged period of time in addition to a guaranteed full return on your initial investment at the time the bond matures, assuming the company or government in question is still around to fulfill those bonds.

If you purchase a bond, instead of becoming a partial owner of a company as you would if you purchased a stock, you are instead becoming a creditor to the issuer of the bond. If this is a local or national government, then odds are you do not have to worry about the debtor vanishing in the night which makes these types of bonds practically risk free as long as you can wait around for them to mature and can deal with the lower than the standard 7 percent return on your investment. Rather, 4 or 5 percent is the average for these types of investments, though companies with a shakier record might offer as much as 10 percent return, though the odds that they will be around to repay what they owe you can be quite slim. However, if the company does go bankrupt then know that you will be paid out before those who are just stockholders will with any available funds.

Oil: To the uninitiated, the oil market can seem extremely confusing as it is prone to dramatic price fluctuations, sometimes on a daily basis. When it comes to influences that affect the price of oil, the biggest in terms of supply is known as the Organization of Petroleum Exporting Countries (OPEC), which supplies more than 80 million barrels of oil each day. This is currently at pace with the worldwide demand, though emerging economies mean that this might not remain the case in the future.

When it comes to investing in oil, those who are looking to capitalize on this ever fluctuating market have several options. Perhaps the simplest is to purchase stocks in companies that drill for oil or companies that are ancillary to the oil business. Additionally, there are several types of mutual funds that focus on stocks in the energy market as well. If you are interested in getting some more direct oil company exposure, you could instead invest in either an exchange traded fund or an exchange traded note, either of which would allow you to invest in oil futures rather than stocks. Futures stick more closely to the price of oil directly than the related energy stocks do, providing an avenue for investment that is not tied to the traditional market.

If you are planning on investing in this market, it is important to do a thorough analysis of any of the companies in question beforehand, paying special attention to how the company specifically turns a profit. Regardless of the details, it is important to understand the cycle of boom and bust inherent in these types of businesses and to always have a clear idea of what part of the cycle the company you are considering investing in is currently in.

Gold: As gold has been prized by civilizations going back beyond recorded history, it is perhaps unsurprising that it is known to come in numerous different forms. Gold's most well-known form is gold bullion, commonly known as gold bars. Gold bars come in different shapes and sizes, which makes some easier to buy and sell than others. Additionally, there are a large number of gold coins in circulation in the US as they have been issued by governments for millennia as well. If you are planning on investing in gold you can typically expect to pay about 5 percent more than what the gold you are purchasing is currently worth.

When it comes to purchasing gold, the biggest benefit is that it is very rare for it ever to decrease in value and you know that you will always be able to find a buyer for your investment when the time is right. Additionally, you will know you will be able to find a comparable seller practically anywhere in the world as the price for gold is fairly stable worldwide. Additionally, you can find gold amounts to fit any investment size, in practically any city around the world. If you do decide to pursue this course of action, however, it is important to keep in mind that if you happen to come across gold bars or coins that appear exceptionally old it is always going to be in your best interest to have these items appraised as they can easily be worth much more than the price of the gold itself in the hands of the right collector.

Real Estate: When it comes to investing in real estate, potential investors have a wide variety of options depending on how hands on they wish to be with their investment. What's more, all types of real estate investment are virtually guaranteed to make at least the industry average 7 percent return on their investment, assuming the market doesn't take one of its infrequent nose dives in the interim. Passive real estate investment can take the form of rental properties that are managed via a property management service, real estate investment trusts which are essential stocks for real estate investment, or wholesaling property.

Rental properties are always an attractive option because you know that the property is increasing in value in the long term, while you still make a profit in the short term. Plus, there is nothing like owning an investment that you can physically touch, see and feel. REITs were designed to allow those with relatively limited financial resources to take advantage of the ownership of larger properties including things like shopping centers, office buildings and hotels. Investors buy into specific REITs and receive a return on their investment equal to the size of the share that they own. Finally, wholesaling property is similar to flipping a property, except without any of the renovation work. In this investment scenario you find a property that has potential, arrange to buy it for a profitable price and then sell that contract to someone who actually follows through on the work, plus several thousand dollars for your time.

Chapter 5: Managing Risk

When it comes to ensuring that you are able to successfully manage the risk that comes along with any of your investments effectively, the first thing you are going to want to do is ensure that you are following your own personalized investment plan in order to prevent yourself from going off book in times of crisis. It is important to keep in mind that having a plan is one thing, sticking with it is another entirely. If you are going to manage your risk properly you are going to need to ensure you have the mental determination and dedication to stick to your plan even if your emotions are urging you to do something else in the moment.

Start with a self-evaluation: The first step to ensuring that you manage the risk inherent in any investments that you do make correctly is to understand exactly what you are working with in terms of personal strengths and weaknesses as well as any external challenges you might be facing in terms of limits on your time or resources. When it comes to evaluating yourself it is important to use an analytical lens and be honest about what you find. There are few character flaws that cannot be properly mitigated using careful planning, but you need to come to terms with what those flaws are before you can work to fix them. Likewise, you need to be aware of the limitations you have on your time and your resources so that you can find an investment plan that works within those guidelines.

While many new investors don't like everything that they find and feel like they can try something that worked for someone else instead, the truth of the matter is that without clearly defining your weaknesses you have no idea what to compensate for. If you are interested in doing more than simply going into a given investment completely blind, then you are going to want to be honest in your self-evaluation up front so that you can ensure you use your strengths as effectively as possible in an effort to mitigate any weaknesses.

Consider how much risk you can realistically handle: The amount of risk that is acceptable for a given investment opportunity is going to vary from person to person based on several factors including the amount of investment capital that you have available to work with as well as how long you have to invest before you want to start seeing substantial results. A general rule of thumb is that any single investment should never exceed more than a total of 5 percent of the full amount you have available to invest to keep losses from staking up to an unfortunate degree in an extremely quick fashion. Furthermore, you are going to want to shoot for at least a 300 percent return on any investments that you make to ensure it is always going to be worth your time, if nothing else.

When you put those two numbers together, you have what is known as the ratio of risk/reward which can be found by determining how much you expect to make on a given investment and then dividing that number by the total amount you expect to make in the process. When working through this equation you are going to want to ensure that the number you come up with is always going to be higher than 3 to ensure you are getting your money's worth with each investment. It is important to remember that this equation doesn't show how likely an investment is going to end in your favor, simply what the results would be like if things go your way.

To find what your tolerance to risk is then all you need to do is determine what your investment parameters are and what an acceptable risk/reward ratio looks like to you. The less time you have to let investments come to fruition, the greater the risk you are going to need to employee to ensure that things work out in the time frame you are hoping they will. If that amount of risk seems too high to you, your only options are to put more money down up front or extend the timeframe, otherwise the risk is going to stay right where it is at.

Know what you are getting into: Once you have a general idea of how much risk you find acceptable, the next thing you are going to want to do is lots of research on the various types of investments and how likely each one is to return results that are within your relative level of risk acceptance. It doesn't matter if there are other types of investments that offer better returns, if the level of risk doesn't line up, you will only be doing yourself more harm than good if you proceed with something that is riskier than you are actually comfortable with.

Always have an exit strategy: One of the keys to investing successfully is always having a clear exit strategy to ensure that you can bail on a given investment the instant it turns in a direction that you no longer find profitable. No two types of investment are ever going to have the same exit strategy which is why it is important to always know what yours is going to be if you want to ensure you keep as much of the profits you made on the investment in the first place as possible. It is important to never get personally attached to specific investments as this will only lead to disaster.

Specifically, doing so will often lead to instances where it seems as though the best choice is to hold onto the investment in hopes that it will eventually turn around once more and head back in the opposite direction. The truth of the matter is that this type of movement rarely, if ever happens and hoping for it is only going to cost you more money in the long run. You will earn more in the long run by cutting your losses as soon as possible than by holding out, guaranteed.

Stick to the plan: Once you have a general idea of what your ideal amount of risk is, it is important to stick to compatible investments with lase like precision. The most profitable type of investments are those made with clear entry and exit points that are then carried out with computer like focus. Only by focusing on the plan that you come up with to the exclusion of all else will you be able to reliably find success in investing month after month and year after year until you claim the level of financial security that is yours by right.

Chapter 6: Setting the Right Goals

If you ever hope to reach a point in time where you can stop thinking about the goals you have set for the future and start enjoying what you have accomplished up to that point, you are going to want to ensure you are setting the right goals at every stage of the process. When it comes to determining if the goals that you set are the right ones for your needs you are going to need to ensure all of your goals are what are known as SMART goals. Additionally, you are going to want to ensure that you always have goals that you are actively pursuing in both the short and the long term in order to gurantee that you are always working towards your goal of financial security in as many different ways as possible.

S is for Specific: First and foremost, it is important that you always pick goals that are specific so that you can always know whether or not you are actually on track with the goal you have chosen. This means you are going to want to have a goal that has a clearly defined state for success as well as failure as otherwise it will be difficult for you to know when the goal has been accomplished.

When it comes to choosing goals that are specific, you are going to want to ensure that you can clearly determine who will help you complete the goal, where the goal will need to be completed at, when the goal will be completed and anything that can stop the goal from being completed. Only by answering all of these questions will you know if you have chosen a truly specific goal.

M is for Measurable: A goal can be said to be measurable if it can be clearly defined as being somewhere between a clearly defined set of points. One of these points should be a clear indication of success and the other should be a clear indicator of failure. When you are first starting out with investing it is important to seek out goals that will allow you to clearly determine if you are currently drifting from the end goal in question. Regularly measuring and keeping tabs on your progress will ensure that you not only start off strong, but you keep up the good work for a prolonged period of time as well. Keeping goals measurable means setting internal due dates and deadlines for sections of the overall goal as well.

A is for Attainable: A good goal is not only specific and measurable; it is realistically attainable as well. All the planning and measuring in the world will never do you any good if you have decided to work towards a goal that is never going to be able to be achieved, no matter what. While setting a goal to be a billionaire might help motivate you to try great things, if you are not already a millionaire then it is too pie in the sky to realistically attempt to approach in the moment. If the goal you are working for doesn't seem realistically attainable you will find it much harder to focus on it with the real determination you are going to need to see any goal through to completion, making it even more unlikely you are going to be able to attain it still. Stick with goals that remain in the realm of possibility for the best results.

R is for Relevant: When it comes to setting goals to improve your financial outlook on life, it is important that you start with goals that will have the most noticeable effect on your day to day life at first, and then work towards more abstract goals from there. This type of approach will have numerous benefits in both the short and the long term, ultimately culminating in a mental state that is clear of distractions and more accurately able to focus on the long term results you need to see true financial freedom.

When you are first starting out, choosing goals that will have the most immediate impact on your current situation will not only make it easier to focus on other tasks down the line once the current distractions are out of the way, it will also teach your brain to associate hard work and dedication with successfully completing goals. This, in turn, will make it easier for you to commit to more difficult or complicated goals in the long term as you will have a historical reason to equate hard work and dedication with success.

T is for Timely: Studies show that the human mind is more likely to actively engage in problem solving behaviors when there is a time limit involved for the successful completion of the task in question. What this means for the goals you are setting for yourself is that if you have a firm completion date in mind for when you want to have reached your goal then you will work harder in the period leading up to that date. This means you are going to want to pick completion dates that are strict enough to truly motivate you to do whatever it is you have in mind, while at the same time not being so strict that there is no realistic way that you can complete the task in question on time. The goal here is to throw a little extra hustle into your step, not force you to keep a grueling schedule, ensure you can always meet the schedule you set for the best results.

Conclusion

Thank for making it through to the end of *Financial Advice: The Top Building Blocks to Personal Wealth and Financial Independence*, let's hope it was informative and able to provide you with all of the tools you need to start to achieve your financial goals whatever it is that they may be specifically. Just because you've finished this book doesn't mean there is nothing left to learn on the topic, however, expanding your horizons is the only way to find the mastery you seek.

Remember, while understanding the basics associated with creating a path to financial independence and personal wealth is an important first step, it is just that, and if you plan on acting on what you have learned then there will be many more between now and the time that you reach the level of wealth that gets you to the point where you are truly financially independent. The step that is immediately in front of you comes with truly understanding the ins and outs of the many types of investment opportunities that are available to you as well as deciding which one suits you the most so that you can move forward as effectively as possible.

Choosing the type of investment that suits your needs is a matter of consulting your personalized investment plan as well as your goals in order to determine what exactly you are going to need to do to get your act together when it comes to creating your financially independent future. As you undertake this journey it is important that you do so with the understanding that it is not going to be quick and easy but rather one that will take months and years of planning and hard work in order to pull of successfully. The results are undoubtedly worth it, however, you just have to want it bad enough to make your dream into a reality. Financial freedom is a marathon, not a sprint, what are you waiting for? It is time to get started.

Finally, if you found this book useful in anyway, a review on Amazon is always appreciated!

Description

Current estimates put the amount required to retire successfully at $500,000 in the bank, despite the fact that more than 60 percent of Americans are currently living paycheck to paycheck and saving less than 2 percent of their total yearly income. If you are currently part of that 60 percent, it can be easy to feel overwhelmed when it comes to getting your finances in order and developing true financial independence but it doesn't have to be and *Financial Advice: The Top Building Blocks to Personal Wealth and Financial Independence* can provide you with the tools to stop thinking about improving your lot in life and to start actually doing it.

When it comes to achieving financial independence, it is easy for those who are on the outside looking in to assume there is some universal secret that is keeping them forever in their place. The reality of the situation is that instead of there being one big secret, there are numerous small differences between those who are financially secure and those who are forever living paycheck to paycheck. This starts with mindset that those who are financially independent cultivate and the habits that they tend to exhibit which is why these facets of the dichotomy between the financially secure and those who are struggling are detailed in depth inside. You will also learn how to work the system like a millionaire by putting the tax code to work for you and ensuring that every investment works with, not against inflation.

Becoming financially secure is all about investing properly which is why there are multiple chapters that are spent on determining the right type of investment for you, creating a personalized investment plan and choosing goals that will lead to the types of results that you are looking for. The biggest difference between those that are financially independent and those that aren't is mindset, those who are financially secure act while those who live paycheck to paycheck dream of one day getting their act together. Adopt the mindset of the financially secure, buy this book today!

Inside you will find

- The four major differences that separate the thought process of those that are financially successful from those who aren't
- Nontaxable sources of income you can utilize to ensure you don't have to pay the federal government more than your fair share
- Taxation credits and deductions you might not even know you qualify for
- The secret to hedging an investing successfully using inflation
- Everything you need to know to get started investigating stocks, bonds, real estate, gold and more
- The best way to create a personalized trading plan to minimize risk
- Easy ways to set SMART goals that you can guarantee have a chance of coming true
- **And more...**

www.ingramcontent.com/pod-product-compliance
Lightning Source LLC
Chambersburg PA
CBHW061239180526
45170CB00003B/1362